LYN LIFSHIN
FOR THE ROSES

Some poems in this book have appeared in the following publications, sometimes in somewhat different form:

Caliban	*Presa*
Gargoyle	*Innisfree*
Lips	*MgVersion*
Yellow Mama	

FOR THE ROSES

PREFACE

It had to be in the mid-seventies when, just divorced, Joni Mitchell's blues echoed mine so wildly. Except for two CDs, someone knowing I was thinking of the project got me, I have just stacks of her LPs, their slightly musty, covers frayed a little in a house I'm rarely in. I think of myself still in those rooms, waiting for a lover to drive up. It's like a museum, a freeze frame the way poems and songs, especially Joni's, can be: a nostalgic, sadly gorgeous sliver of what isn't, was, or maybe couldn't be.

This past summer, along with an assignment for something that often seemed a chore, came the chance to go back and listen to Joni's music and words again. It was an exquisite thrill.

On one of my reading tours of California, someone who knew a young writer had a hero-crush on two people, Joni Mitchell and me, made up an elaborate plan: he would be warned of a surprise.

When we showed up at his house, I might as well have been Joni. He was so overwhelmed he could only stare, frozen.

When I read Joni's words, so often they seem like my words: the glittery sadness, the wanting. As I write this, I've glanced through my own books and see phrases from her songs. By accident or allusion, I have used similar wording. So many about past loves, the lovers that are gone but haunt me on TV, in the media, in dreams. I have files of poems about a man whom women worshiped who hosted all-night radio. Others went on to earn prestigious prizes, awards, and grants. Seeing their faces or hearing their voices in memory brought on a melancholy. We crave, we receive, we let slip. "Blue," "loss," "roses," "remember," and what you hear in the wind at night stud my poems as well as her lyrics.

I love her song, *For the Roses*. I love the record jacket. In the cover photo, she is wearing velvet and boots as I so often did (and still do). We both paint, as reclusive as writing. I, too, started as an art major, was sure that would be what I needed to do. I love her impressionist drawings. I draw flowers bright, bold, but never quite connected to the stem. Impressionistic—a little crazy. You can see some of them on my website (www.lynlifshin.com).

She came from the steppes of Canada and I came down from the hills of Vermont. I learned from her that an outsider can use what she creates to ease pain. Verbs and paint were beautiful masks. I thought of her as a sister. Her songs are clearly poems: suggestive and magical with enough left out, forcing me as a listener to make my own leaps. I love what is left out and if I find too much is there, I try to change it. The cadence, the sensuality, the juxtaposition of nature and emotion. I yearned to create strong images like "the moon swept down the black water/like an empty spotlight."

I also love *For the Roses* because my real name is Rosalyn and my Hebrew name is Raisel Devora, Deborah of the roses. For most of my life I've worn some scent: Tea Rose, White Rose, Rose the One, Bulgarian Rose, Rashmi Rose, White Rose, Drole de Rose, Damask Rose, Tuber Rose, Southampton Rose (a true favorite now gone for years), Mistral Rose, Joy. Redolent of Bulgarian attar, intoxicating (to me, at least). Rose scents carry the most evocative names: Le Pot Aux Roses, Rose Oud, Secrets de Rose, Prima Ballerina, Parfume d'Empire, Bouton de Rose, Amber Rose, Abbey Rose, Twilight Rose, Kimona Rose, Ombre Rose Canabis Rose, Damascena, Rose Barbare, Paris Rose, Shisedo's Rose, By the Banks of Rose, Les Palms of Rosine, Rose Damascena, Valentino Rock 'n' Rose, Yosh Winter Rose, Velvet and Sweet Oea's Jewelry of Heaven, Red Flower Guaiac, Roja Dove Scandal, Forbidden Rose, Baby Rose Jeans, Woman in Rose, Cabotine Rose, Rose the One. So many names for intoxication.

I nearly called a recent book *Dark Rose*—and I imagine there may not be a single book or chapbook of mine without the word in at least one poem. With each avatar I imagine Joni fascinated with all it suggests.

For Joni, then, the rose arrangement given the winner of the Kentucky Derby, *The Last Rose of Summer, Abby's Irish Rose,* the blood of Christ, the ballet *Specter of the Rose,* the blue of a woman's body after orgasm, the rose of sexual organs: cock head, nipples, cunt. *Rosebud,* William Randolph Hearst's pet name for his mistress's clitoris.

Of course all flowers die but somehow the dying rose, seems to have that mix of excruciating beauty and then its loss. My first corsage—a yellow rose. The rose Allen Ginsberg gave me—I carried it through airports and everyone gasped "roses" but it was the Tea Rose I was wearing. Of course I chose roses for sterling, often dress in rose. I still have my rose sixteenth birthday party dress and often wear it. And I've used it to mark my scent in a new lover's blue sheets.

Every part of this song connects to some snapshot in my life. Each makes me remember things I hadn't thought of in years. Vivid as the smell of the roses, I'm drawn to how she writes of sadness, transience but also the beauty that comes from this, the fierceness. Trieste and joy—as if the joy depends on what dark things one has gone through. I am drawn to her addiction to love, her aching for something she could hold, holds me. Her ribbons of melancholy, her sense of what is so broken it catches the light, finds and makes exquisite beauty in wreckage like those "torn bottles the ocean's turned to sea glass jewels," the sense that "what dissolves behind you in the rearview mirror remains long enough to haunt you" like her trees—slashes of wild paint shivering in a naked row: such exquisite beauty out of what is torn.   —LYN LIFSHIN

FOR THE ROSES

I think of her watching the
last rose petals on a
day like today, say deep
August, browning like
an old rubber doll
she might have left
in an attic in Canada.
I think of her pressing
skin against glass, a sense
of summertime falling,
that sense of fall
that that Sylvia Plath
wrote of. Or maybe some
freeze frame of what
is going, moving on.
I see her pale arms,
sea mist velvet jeans
hugging hips that
never will not be boyish.
In the wind, gone
voices move close
to her cheek bones. In
this frame she could be in
a fancy 30's gown. Some
thing is raw, some thing
is broken. It has to be
a full moon
etching black water.
She has to know that
from what is torn

and scarred, some
thing almost too
exquisitely beautiful
is already stirring,
some thing dark
as coal becoming
diamond, insistent,
dying to be born

SOMETIMES I THINK OF HER

as a wild foal, hardly
touching down in prairie
grass, Saskatchewan. Or a
sea nymph, her gaze
glued to the deepest
emerald wave, a Silkie
luring men she can't stay
with long. There she
is, on a seaweed jeweled
rock, her songs, ribbons
of melancholy lassoing you,
pulling on your heart.
Some say Bessie Smith
left even or especially good
men to have something
to make her songs
burn the hottest blues. I
think of Joni knowing
what can't stay, what is so
broken it catches the
light like torn bottles
the ocean's turned
to sea glass jewels, that
what dissolves behind you in the rear
view mirror haunts,
knife-like as her trees,
slashes of wild paint

shivering in a naked row,
such exquisite beauty
in wreckage

FOR THE ROSES

I wore Tea Rose and
often a black rose
in my hair that summer,
symbol of freedom,
a nod to the White Rose,
the German girl who
protesting the Nazis,
gave her skin, her lips
and heart, her life. I was
flying coast to coast
to read, coming back
to an alone house. Named
for the rose, for a aunt
adventurous as Joni,
who danced in flames,
I dressed in rose. Deborah
of the roses. The stories
about her whispered by
grown ups behind stained
glass doors. Who wouldn't
expect roses in my poems?
White rose, Bulgarian
rose. When I walked thru
airports with a white
rose from Allen Ginsberg
everyone whispered, "roses."
But it was the rose scent
perfuming the air from my
body. You could almost
hear, as even now I can

almost feel the one who
touched me on that
coast, what Joni heard
in the wind, the end
of, the chilly now,
the last face to face

CHINESE CAFÉ
UNCHAINED MELODY

I think of Joni, remembering
back in the old home town,
in some back seat, her green
check dress wrinkling a
long time as things inside
unchained were saying yes,
yes. And she did. I think
of her remembering
how she chose a name
for the girl she couldn't keep.
Does she think of her
blue eyes I wonder, so many
years later. Is some part
of her still a child with a child
pretending. She wanted
green, so often wears
green, is some how part of
her still, sad and sorry.
Unchained, unchained,
hungering so for a long time
for your touch, a touch

READING SONG
TO A SEA GULL

When I read about the
photo retouch expert in
Japan, taking what's
blurred and faded, torn,
assumed lost and how
removed from debris,
as I've pulled some of
Joni's songs from a
dark room in the house
I'm rarely in, what
was, blooms again, brings
back the most vivid
memories. I listen again
to her words, the
lyrics raw and direct,
chunks of what I
thought I'd lost and I'm
astonished, as those
locals in Japan who come
to look thru photos that
were found, cleaned
so they can hold
what they no longer
have, touch, bury
themselves in

CACTUS TREE

"raw and direct, what in
her life is really happening."
I read this of a new young
star. Someone says she
makes you feel like she's
your best friend, that she's
gone thru hell and come
out as a beauty, her
losses honed into words
that touch you. Of course
she reminds me of Joni
pulling from the pain
of those men who called
her from the harbor,
kissed her with their
freedom, what
shimmers like light
thru stained glass. How
she transforms the
blackness, holes in the
air, the ache. I think
of her making jewels
from those who
climbed mountains,
calling out her name,
leaving their stain,
of her stalking images
of dreams flying with sea
gulls and sand castles,
worlds they can't share.

Sand castles crumble.
From what isn't said
she spins magic,
words that hold you,
will be enough to
keep you as long as
you long to

SONG FOR SHARON

I think of women
so close to the line,
so close to letting
go. So far from
satisfaction. Women
dreaming of a lace
wedding dress,
dreaming of
losing futility. I
think of Joni's
words that tangle,
that craziness of
wanting a family
with horses, children
and then running,
as if everything that
could bring comfort
could be a jail.
Some suggest have
children, help
the poor, spend some
time on ecology.
I imagine her feeling
it's not enough,
how the woman in
the song wants
another lover. How
many women haven't
worn lace tights
under ripped

slim jeans. But I'm
thinking it is just these
damsels in distress,
not the prom queens
and the voted
most popular who
become Amazon
women maybe because
they have no choice
word magicians
who can touch you,
hypnotize you
in a spell no
one else can

FOR THE ROSES

the way I scrawl my name,
the petals that don't
connect to any center.
I felt like that that
summer, packing and
unpacking my head,
alone in a hotel room
drifting like milkweed
dust. Rose on my wrist
and nipples. I think of
Joni, her blonde hair, a
fan on the rocks of the
Pacific miles from where
an ex-con poet sent me
keys to a hide-away. He
might as well have
been a rock star, Joni's
rock n roll man,
the kind any blond would
flip her hair for, fall
and follow home. A man
you can't hold long or
count on. Back in my room
I played her songs
over and over as moths
brushed the August
screens and berries
glistened. It was so still,

so much seemed too
good to waste and
I wasn't even blonde
to the bone yet

FOR THE ROSES

When I see hers
sprawled across the album,
explosive brush strokes,
guava, blood and green,
her wild petals not
connected to any
stem. I can't help but
feel those slashes
of light in your poems,
how sometimes if seems
your words could be mine.
I've heard those lost
lovers in the wind. Maybe
I heard then last night
when I couldn't
sleep. I think of the
photograph of you with
a rose in your hair. You
could be my sister those
nights when I am the
rose I was named
for, Raisel Devora.
And why wouldn't some
one pierced by words,
turn addict for a
sense rare as Tea Rose
or Rashimi rose incense.
Those lovers, like
applause: I found them
addictive too. I think of you

crisscrossing the country,
a cigarette dangling,
leather and suede,
tawny earth colors
(you could find in my
closet), eyes few would ever
be as blue as. Aching for
something you can't
still hold and knowing
from that raw wound, pain
and piercing beauty explodes

FOR THE ROSES

sometimes what stays
is the odd way one
said "Albany." Or
another's print on the
wall no paint hides.
You hear "honey"
in the wind. So few
called me that
many years. As in
her song, that
sound, like applause,
face to face. Tristes
and joy. I can feel
her feeling it. Some
times what stays
is the fog the
day after, a voice
on the radio like
skin, days when her
words were like
lips on the air. No
more shiny hot nights
of rose petals, but
that touch that will
stay, last if it has to, as
long as your
heart beats

LET THE WIND CARRY ME

like tumbleweed, like
milkweed. Wind
blown, drifting between
hands. *Oh she's a
free spirit* boys use to
sing to me too, shaking
their head. No one
can hold her. My mother
tried to, my father didn't
care. Joni knew you
could be so drawn
and quartered. Wanting
a home with candles
around the door,
wanting a man who'd
be there to hold her and
then packing in the
night, eloping alone with
strangeness in a short
skirt and heels, fuck me
shoes and a hooker
sequin mini: a mask, a
moat only the wind catches

ROSES, BLUE

when I go back and
look at those poems,
its as if Joni
dabbled in them.
A little jazz, a
blues riff. I think
of the woman on
the metro, sobbing.
I think of rain.
I think of roses.
Of blues my baby
left me. I think
of Joni's woman
with her Tarot cards
and tears, of all
things that did not,
could not happen,
more haunting than
so much that did

TIN ANGEL

her words are my
words: "tarnishes,"
"beads" tapestries."
I think she's my
doppelganger with
her letters from
across the seas
and her roses
dipped in sealing
wax. Was there
something in the
water those rose
and butterfly years?
The white rose
Alan Ginsberg
gave me flattened
in a Shakespeare
Folio before wax
caked its leaves
could have been one
her tin angel sent.
The columbine
I planted in the
house I'm rarely in,
color of her lips,
her crying. I too sat
in a Blecker St Café.
I used "tarnish" over
and over that year

FOR THE ROSES

when I hear butterflies
and lilac sprays, the
glitter, the what she
heard in the wind,
a fierce lullaby.
I think of Virginia
Woolf keeping
fragments, scraps of
images, tossed
them in a drawer. I
think if I cut lines
from a random
number of songs,
Chelsea Morning,
California and esp.
Blue, color that
leaks thru my writing
and put, like slices
of colored glass
or velvet squares from
a quilt into kaleidoscopes,
into a bedroom drawer
and waited to see
what would coalesce,
each time I dipped
the verbs would
keep changing and I
don't think I could
tell Mitchell's
words from mine

CALIFORNIA

It was definitely California,
bougainvillea breaking
out like purple stars.
Not Paris, not Africa.
Jet lagged, coming from
the snow, heat and
light like a drug and my
own words in the trunk.
Not there from Los Vegas
or a Grecian Isle but
escaping lovers I could
not stay with too. I didn't
think anyone did the
goat dance but I wish
someone had a camera.
I suppose we had a little
wine because some
one planned what they were
sure would give a sad
eyed man a treat, put
back his smile. Another
said he had two ladies,
two women he swore he'd
always love, two
women whose faces filled
the rooms in his tiny house:
posters, albums, books.
It was wild. One was
Joni, the other me. Warned
of the surprise, the man's

face went snow standing at
the window. I was high
on his being as happy
it was me. I think they told
him it would be one
of us. Probably I wore
madras or tie-dyed. My long
hair sleek as Joni's. I
was wearing my spider
medallion. I wasn't used to
such a shy fan, too shy
to come to the door. I too
was strung out on another man.
I had a week or two to
hang around. He wasn't
the first to be afraid to talk
to me at a reading, to run
out before the end. All that
time I thought of Joni,
her songs in my hair, my
own pretty strangers
and the bad news of war
and now I wonder if
he often thinks of
both of us

MICHAEL FROM MOUNTAINS

I think of her
wanting to retreat,
stop touring. I
imagine her exhaustion,
think of Edna St
Vincent Millay feeling
like a hooker
going to read. Who
doesn't get sick of
tour? "Which is the real"
they howl? What's
true? Who's the
man in the lyrics and
did he do what
you wrote he did? I
think of 30 men sure they
were the one in a
certain poem about none
of them. Who would
not want to escape, have
someone wake you
up with sweets
and roses, take you
out in the rain
in a yellow slicker? Who
doesn't want cats
running when you turn
the key? A sun in
the painting
that smiles?

LUCKY GIRL

one song where the
blues are mixed
with sun and if you
painted this poem
it would be green,
mellow. After a
litany of men she
loved but never
trusted with their
shy lover eyes, their
big bad bedroom
eyes. Now she's a
lucky girl, a sunny girl
a no longer treated
like a toy girl but
a truly lucky
girl whose lover
makes night
crawling disappear

NIGHT IN THE CITY

I think of her deciding to retire,
wild for stillness, an
escape from the crowds,
needing to go inside
herself. She couldn't just
sing the same songs,
the thrill of fame
tarnishing, being a
traveling lady
losing its glow. She
must have been tired of so
many places to come
from, places to
go and wanted to get
out and meet people, not
be like a bird in a
cage with a
spotlight on her.
She wanted to take off, run
laughing with no one
to meet, wanted
music spilling into the
street, in Europe,
in France, Spain and
Greece, dulcimers
in the night breeze instead
of strangers clapping

OUT OF THE CITY
AND DOWN TO THE SEA SIDE

with her dulcimers, her
songs. Writing at night.
Once she could write
anywhere. Once she
was invisible as blown
seeds. Once she could
write on sand, under
cypress. Once no one
cared "who's that
about." Sometimes
she'd write something
down and think "Oh
I like how the words
sound but it doesn't
say anything." Some
times friends come and
listen to her sing. If
they love her songs, it's
better than drugs
or gin. Sometimes she
felt like a hippie goddess
rocking rhythms while
they're waiting
with candles in the
window. Sometimes
what she's feeling
is not anything a poet
can sing

THE DAWN TRADER

I think of her past cities
and towns listening to
songs the rigging makes,
how the sea's verbs
paint damp sand. Peridots
and periwinkle glisten
like new elegant words.
Roll of the harbor wake.
Splashes of irony.
When she walks out
past the spray, perfect
images move thru
her fingers. Her hair in
sea wind, city satins
left at home. Sunlight and
dolphins, her poems
from sea dreams can't
help but makes us feel we
are not alone

THE PIRATE OF PENANCE

I think of those pirate men
coming in the night
with the broken leg and
broken promises. I
think of ladies dancing
in bars, sure they
can lasso and conquer men
who won't stay the night.
Love, fleeting as
fame, as groupies
dying for you, leaving
you drowning. Words
that will sting,
sails unfurling like fans who
bring silk and sandal
wood and Persian
lace, come to
port for pleasure,
leave you drowning

CACTUS TREE

I think of her wanting to
drive across country to
Maine. A relief there
wasn't e-mail. Too many
letters coming too soon.
Too many men with beads
from California, their
amber stones and green.
I know those California
ghosts with their dreams
and stories calling
from the sea, kissing
her with their freedom.
I think of men busy
being free, of poets
staggering from the west
coast with broken shoes
and lies. Who hasn't
been torn by the night
mare of having a family
and not having a family. I
think of men calling
out her name, hoping she
can hear them. Men
missing in the forest or
sending letters, waiting for
a reply. I've known too
many men like that,
been that lady in the city
thinking she loved

them all. I've gotten those
medals from a man who
is bleeding from a
war, who only means
to please but will
lose her if they follow

I THINK OF HER AS AMELIA

driving into blackness alone,
daring and driven,
leaving vapor trails.
On the run—
you can't tell if it is
toward or away from
what could hold her.
Alone with her
own thoughts, a comfort,
an ice pick. Hexagons
of what she's
flung from trailing
like hieroglyphs. No one
can read her. Wild
flying engines sing a song
so wild and blue it
blurs the night. No one
can really tell her
where to go
and she'll never know
until she gets there.
Her hand on the wheel
wishing who knows who was
there beside her. Is she
daydreaming Icarus?
half wishing the sky or
sea would gulp her?

COYOTE

I think of her up
all night in the studio,
think of the one she
held now brushing out
a brood mare's tail.
If you don't feel her
aloneness, don't feel
how close to the
bone and skin and eyes
you can get and still
feel so alone,
you don't feel.
Some nights scorch
memory like her
farmhouse burning
down. I'm in my old
house where a dead
love's hand print
on the gray wall under
layers of paint
still sucks on me.
No matter those ghosts
had a woman at
home, another down
the highway. Too
many go for these men
no one can tame
with their pills and

powder, holding on to
your scent while
beckoning another

BLUE MOTEL ROOM

the beauty of the
word "cellophane."
I think of the world
thru it. Slick black
cellophane, like
scrim where the
actors are shapes,
mysterious, shifting.
Makes me think of
blue sheets in a
room like a blue
motel. I wore bluer
lace bikinis. His
eyes the bluest.
She reminds me if
I'd been in Savannah
there'd have been
pouring rain and
my blues would have
tattooed you

DON JUAN'S
RECKLESS DAUGHTER

hitching into mystery,
jiving in the mountains.
I think of her dancing
to an old juke box, a
gold snake on her wrist,
old ghosts, lips of
serpents who love the
whiskey bars. I imagine
the wind in her blondeness
on the prairie. I think of
her restless in honky
tonks, in lace. I think of
those shadows that
feel like touching,
of shadows that feel
like skin. Now all she
wants since she can't
have you is for you
to shiver, put her on your
danger list

NOTHING CAN BE DONE

I think of Joni, no longer the
waif with perfect skin,
frozen lake eyes. I think of
her remembering when
her words hit high on
Billboard, the covers of
Rolling Stone. Young babes,
who isn't wild for them?
They don't even know. I
think of Joni writing
how the heart is a lonely
gun, maybe alone before a
mirror, skin not the skin
it was, hair more gray
than blonde. Men she held
like milkweed dust.
Too many women feel
it's too late to start again
but even when nothing can be
done, Joni makes a
song of it

THE GALLERY

the sister I never had
seems to pose in
clothes I swear came
out of my closet. Her
velvets, leather and
lace. If we were
framed in a gallery you
might think we were
twins. You can see
past the hair in our
faces, our haunting eyes,
how we're haunted
by falling for too
many men, wrong
men, sure we gave all
our pretty years to.
"It's not you, it's me," a
litany that's stained
both our skins. And do
sisters often go after
the men too many
others want?

ELECTRICITY

It was when the power
went down and then his
wild electricity. It
was the night
Challenger flared and
flamed, turned ash
as so much did. But
that's another story.
Upstate N.Y, iced trees
crashed wires. Even
by noon it kept
getting colder. Cherry
wood burning scented
my long red hair, scorched
an old boyfriend's
warm up clothes. He's
dead now and the one just
starting a circuit to
my heart. The shuttle
news played a
blues riff into darkness.
The astronauts' hair,
dust in the stars. I was
under more quilts, the
cat near the fire
as ice crystals formed
in the toilet and that
all night talk radio voice
held me thru coldness
as it would when he

was more than
electricity on air.
It all went back to that
night. It was the way
Joni Mitchell would have
remembered some
thing like this

YOU TURN ME ON:
I'M A RADIO.

When he was on air,
he's like air, all I
needed to breathe.
I could turn him on
as he did me from
that first afternoon
driving into those
mountains thru wild
flowers, the leaves
already going
blood. Joni Mitchell
would know autumns
of terror when it feels
warm thru glass but
you know the heat's
going. His voice,
on my way to teach,
his first day and I knew
I had to have him.
Later I'd wait dawns
for him o get off his
all night show, hooked
the radio to the VCR,
I was as hooked on him.
I could tell how much
each woman came on to
him, the change in his
breathing. When he'd
break dates, it was like

driving thru static. He
turned me on and left
me dangling. When the
reception sucked, I
wanted to smash the
radio on icy tiles. I hated
getting hip to his tricks
or racing to the parking
lot before he went on air.
Or knowing I'd come
when he whistled even
when my head said
forget. Like Joni said,
sure the lines at the station
were open but I couldn't
get thru

NOT YET THE BLONDE IN THE BLEACHERS

Still, sometimes, I think Joni Mitchell
was my doppelganger, my other. Of
course it wasn't our voices. I don't
sing, not since an ex-husband giggled
when I took down my old guitar. And
I wasn't the blonde with corn yellow
hair flowing free on beaches waves
crash, naked, wild to plunge into every
thing, at least not yet, waiting on
bleachers, plump as my fat bulky socks
decorated with bells and balls and tinsel,
aching to be asked to dance. But I was
painting as she was in a room with the
door closed as Otter Creek crashed
below the window and I was dreaming
of being on a stage. I was still half the
unknown child but in the same tie dye I
saw her in a photo. Our nights at Club 47,
maybe the wine class she used was
the one I'd use later, already falling
for folk singers years before I'd finally
catch one. How easy those years to give
up a piece of one's soul on the way to
becoming blondes men might want to
dance with. I might have seen her in the
mirror, sliding from man to man, too often
the wrong one with the urge for going.
How often did we both envy Georgia O'
Keeffe, out there in the blue and dusk
desert making beauty out of joy and pain.

"Ebullience and tristesse" someone said
of me but nothing could have described
her better, feeling like she said, a cellophane
wrapper on a pack of cigarettes with
absolutely no secrets from the world,
hardly able to protect her life

SEE YOU SOMETIME

I think of you not
wanting to put your
claws in, imagining
an old love holding
a woman who came
on to you. "Honey"
was what one I never
could hold long, just
feel his skin move
over mine before he'd
crutch away, called
me. Sometimes I feel
you could be my
twin. I'm another
mama lion, not
wanting to change
my name. I don't know
if that's a lie, a line.
But I drove to the
parking lot and I can
see you doing that too,
going to meet a plane,
wild to make clear
you don't want any
thing from this man,
not his name or
money, but just want
to see him again

BAD DREAMS

the way a door opens
in a ghost story, Joni
dreams a bad one. It
blooms, a black tulip,
the dark hawks buzz.
Someone's let her
down. You know the
story. They are the
charms on my anklet,
the blues in the bread.
She says they're good,
little gems come out
of them. You don't
want a Hallmark
card, do you?

REFUGE OF THE ROAD

making up songs and poems
traveling in the car. Fierce
verbs, bits of darkness.
Even on the desert, too
much baggage. "Hejira,"
she says, "was written
mostly traveling in one
car," leaving what dissolves
in the rear view mirror.
Just images of what
almost was. Long hair
blowing, lullaby of
passing towns. Faces blurry
as the first shots from the
moon. It was so hot
in Phoenix peaches rotted
on the way from the store.
Both of us running to
lose the blues. The farther
you get away from what
happened, the clearer
it seems

CAR ON A HILL

when I think of her waiting
for her sugar, listening
to sirens, listening
to the radio, I half believe
she's me waiting for my
real good talker,
waiting in blackness
after his midnight to dawn
radio show. I think
of her feeling hours slide
away. I was waiting
in a pretty nightgown, my
hair more red. Every
one loved him, women
wanted to bring him
Tasty Cakes and
eggs. When I waited in his
blue sheets, Ravena, I
knew he'd have to
show. But in my own house,
where his finger prints
still bleed thru layers of
paint, after such sparks
at the radio station,
after such sweetness in
the dark, I could
just wonder now, too,
where in the city
can that boy be

JUST LIKE THIS TRAIN

it was at an airport in
Albuquerque waiting for
hours. I think how
Joni said she used to
count lovers like railroad
cars. She's what I see
in the mirror, knowing
jealous lovin'll make
you crazy. Was her deep
blue so close to her skin
you can see it? Like
bruises or a blue tree
branching out or the roots
of blue indigo. How
many men did she find
who have no one to
give their love to but were
too broken to take some?
How many nights, wanting
to climb into a train
booth and pull down the
blind?

I THINK I UNDERSTAND

with my own wilderlands.
Reams of poems called
"panic" and "terror. The
black roses that block
the light. She pulls night
out of her and black
diamonds sing, her tongue
on light. No one who
hasn't tasted the deepest
blackness could bring
up such brightness

HELP ME

I've the blues.
Hear her warning.
She's under my
skin again, in
my skin—she
pulls me into her
rhythm. I'm there
with my water
color paints and
ink, not able to
stay within the
lines too. Oh our
blue, blue mountains,
signatures hard
to read. Maybe we
don't quite know
who we are or want
anyone else to.
Flirting and
hurting. Falling and
bawling. Sweet
talking ramblers
and gamblers.
Didn't we date the
same men? The
ones that after
years show up as
we are about
to go on stage

COURT AND SPARK

what does it mean when
each poem of hers feels
like I had written it?
Sometimes its what is
left out like in any blues.
The what isn't there
haunts and staggers and
what of these men taking
up too much room
with their silver tongues,
their mad man's soul.
I don't remember bringing
lost kittens home but
those sea-eyed men
stagger thru my poems
too, fragile and broken, as
exotic cars I can't afford

TROUBLE CHILD

it's his gorgeous language
like silk spun into ribbons,
threads immigrants tied
to those on shore as boats
pulled out and what was
all that mattered got
smaller and smaller and
what held them went
transparent, disappeared.
In so many songs, what's
fragile and could break
has its own luminosity:
the child in a sterilized
room, breaking like the
waves at Malibu

FREE MAN IN PARIS

its those girls, Nabokov
overheard in Paris, "funny,
how they all smell alike,
burnt leaf through what
ever perfume they use.."
Do those girls go after
that kind of free man in
Paris? A dealer of dreams
who goes from café to
cabaret like he flits between
women. It's those men too
many women are after,
wandering Champs d'Elysses?
Is this song, this man a
symbol of the ones who
can walk away telling you
nothing you didn't know
but forgot you knew it

THE LAST TIME
I SAW RICHARD

too many last times
with too many men.
Heard Rolling Stone
did a family tree of
your conquests. Makes
me think of men I've
heard I've looked up
in places I've never
been. I think melancholy,
infinite sadness. I think
your words are mine
sometimes. All those
men with tombstones
in their eyes wanting to
crash your skin. Those
once beauties, good at
pretty lies, running
out of time

ALL I WANT

I think of her traveling,
a traveling woman, a
woman on a lonely
road, the moon in her
eyes. Infinite sadness.
Been there too. And
the interviews: Are
you promiscuous? Do
you write like a girl?
"Poetess" curdles my
ear. "Are you a female
song writer? Is what
you're confessing
really true? and what
do you think of the
young babes selling
more than you do?"
It's not just lost men
who turn Wednesday
blue. I'm at the kitchen
table, record heat and
the sky going gray
as a fog of sadness.
103 in the shade. I can
imagine Joni on the
bleacher waiting for
someone to ask her to
dance and decades later,
still not sure any
one will

ALL I WANT

lines that come like
a gift when you're
in the zone. Ebullient
sadness, traveling
lonely roads,
looking for something.
Lady Lyn, Ladies
of the Canyon. Show
them you won't
expire, a waif
waiting to please.
So many songs of
sadness. Who cares
if introspection's
gone out of style on
these lonely
roads looking
for the key

ALL I WANT

I think of her
on lonely roads,
traveling, wanting,
window shopping
in the rain, blonde
hair graying. I
think of her
wanting a life
like Georgia O
Keeffe, the beauty
of spaces,
blue black tulip.
All she really
wants is to
talk to you

ALL I WANT

so many lonesome roads
writing herself out
of depression. Turbulent
indigo. Sapphire
glitz, comforting her
self with creation.
Star crossed
loves. What you can't
leave. Even a
famous icon scooping
her up in her arms
among the carrots and
the roses was
not enough. Or
singing clear notes
without fear, cheering
up sad teenagers

WHAT I WANT

traveling, looking for a
key. What's wrong
with obsession?
Always upswing
or downswing. Wanting
to have fun, to write
love letters tho
sadness, that
onyx rose, moves
from one
song to the next like the
drip of an iv. "Show
'em you won't
expire. Not
till you burn up
every passion," a
diamond of
ice on the Coachella

ALL I WANT

I think of her on a
lonely road, traveling,
wild to meet O'Keeffe,
waiting in the blue
shadows, waiting in
darkness the first
time, wanting
to take a chance.
Too many women
pick men who'll
make them jealous.
Waiting to be
asked to dance,
desperate to jive.
All we really want,
a riddle, lost key.
But then, the
worlds desperate
consolation of
sadness filling all
the blanks. Words like
feathers floating
over the water, a
flutter as close
as voices on
radio air whose
stories make
a cove

LITTLE GREEN

mysterious as her
story. Or a daughter
given away. Once
a woman wanted
to change her name
to "Gitana" with a
soft g, wanted to
run away with the
gipsies, dance in
blackness, gold
bracelets blindingly
bright, fake jewels
in firelight. Her
father, an illusion,
a ghost, at the end
of the table not
talking years
before any divorce
decree as if it
wasn't there always

CAREY

the strangeness of what's
left out. The magic
names of cities. Devil
dreams of what could
go on for years,
of men who keep
you dancing
in strange cities, the
nights a starry
dome. Who doesn't
remember some
mean old Daddy as
they water the roses
still fresh, still clear,
as her crystal
high soprano. Phantom
lovers, too expensive
to keep except in
songs or poems.
Give her Amsterdam,
give me Mermaid Café
and the most fancy
French cologne,
let us stay stunned
as someone who
sees a man on the
subway with a
ring on his little finger

flash by and makes
up a lifetime
out of it

THIS FLIGHT TO NIGHT

feeling ready in
her shoes. The lights
down here, after
too many readings.
Even Liv Ullmann said
coming home it
seemed life went on
on other houses.
No falling stars to
burn my heart up.
No early star or
northern fire, no sweet
champagne, no lips
to quiet loneliness.
I think of men who've
got the touch so
gentle I get so weak
too. I could dream
of what I didn't have,
darkness everywhere,
flying thru clouds,
hoping to drum one
man out of my life.
Starlight, star bright.
Face to face, I could
not tell him except
on paper where I am
hoping, as she says,
it's better when
we meet again

NATHAN LA FANEER

so many cabs
tearing thru fog
and rain. Strangers
you're trapped with
wanted more
money. Furrowed
eye brows, stink
of smoke crawling
thru traffic on
the way to perform.
I think of one in
Boston who wanted
me to stay the night.
Who knows who
you'll end up
with or where. It's
part of fame, part of
being wanted.
Ghostly garden and
woe, it's part of
the bargain. At least
I got there in time
to go on stage
and my clothes
weren't torn
from me

SONG TO A SEA GULL

who isn't wild for
what they can't share?
For what they can't
can't possess? I think of
Joni wanting to be
as free, away from
concrete beaches,
away from city
lights instead of
stars, away from false
flowers. I think of
her wanting to be away
from microphones
and pills, reviews and
studios. Out of
reach, out of
cry. Just sun on
her shoulders,
wind in her
hair

HEJIRA

that summer of the
American Bicentennial
thru the country,
festivals, music, and
poetry. How many
were with lovers
they knew could
not stay? Sail boats
on the Hudson. Those
journeys taken to
seek refuse from a
dangerous, a terrifying
environment. Gray
days, moody and
 subdued. Writing
from the road, trying
to be ok with not
having a family, as
if anyone truly
has anyone

HIJERA

I think of her riding,
going across country,
too much in the
rear view mirror
and what of the girl
she left behind.
The cold shells,
the cold lips of lovers.
Reckless daughter days.
Brakes as slit guitar
strings. Writing
mostly traveling
in a car, a journey to
seek refuge, wild
for what seemed
dangerous or
wrong to dissolve.
The faster she went,
her foot on the
gas the more lips
and fingers blurred.
She was hot to leave
the petty wars—
who wouldn't lunge
from damaging
lovers, sit in
some café so shell
shock love vanishes.
When I left the
man camping out in

the trees, the ex
con women died for,
I wanted to return
to myself too.
I was that ballroom
girl, snow in me
feathering like
bolts of lace.
Still, sitting in the
Boulder station, I
wanted to believe I was
glad to be
on my own

HEIJIRA

I think of Joni
driving alone past
prairie towns feeling
young, feeling
old. A gray
black mood,
travel fever, snow,
shivering blues
in the pinewoods.
How little lasts
between the forceps
and the stone.
I think of her
shivering at the granite
markers in small
towns of her
self, scratching for
something that
lasts longer
than love

A STRANGE BOY

of course it was
New England but when
I hear of her strange
boy weaving havoc
and grace, only one,
clinging to the past,
fidgeting, maybe
bullied slithered up
before me. Large doe
eyes. He might as
well have had a
skate board in his
head. He walked up
behind me near the
Congregational Church.
He was strange, he
was child like.
He said I was pretty.
He had so many
grants but when he
asked me, said he'd
made the dinner,
slapped my face when I
wouldn't do the dishes,
then sent dozens
of roses. Now I can't
imagine him not
still being the same
strange child holding
me in a confession

booth not far
from the Armenian ladies.
Yes I know how those
feelings come and
go like the pull
of moons on tides, on
our clutching
each other in the
confessional. I think
of her giving a
man clothes and jewelry,
her warm body and
I wonder as I do
about that man last known
to be dazed in the
canyons off the Pacific,
what he is like as
an old man

SONG FOR SHARON

I think of that long white
dress of love. I think of a pale
Mexican dress I lusted for
in Guadalajara, perfect
for my long ironed hair.
If it was lacy, it was a lure.
It was like poems. It was
like using words for skin.
I would have ached for the
long white dress of love. I
think of being that young and
of her in her 20's singing
how first you get your
kisses and then you get your
tears. Her musty LP like
my still white lace spills from
my closet instead of kisses

BLACK CROW

dark blue,
glittery, swooping

dark as any black cat blues,
relentless, restless, reckless

see them in a film
and you know death is coming

black wings, black as
a just tarred road

dark as night mares,
wild for something shiny

I feel those dark wings
under my skin,
blackly purple

I think of one girl
in love with crows,
like a crow herself

darting, driven,
ruthless and shiny

and then, like anything
dark and shimmery

as night,
left in the night

COTTON AVENUE

one of those places
you have to go when
you're young and
your blood is boiling,
ripe, juicy. Summer
fills the air. I think
of Cove Point on
Lake Dunmore. Ashes
now and not even
ashes left but dreams
of those summer nights,
a raspberry sun sinking
into the water and
yes there were
dogs and frogs and
night birds and then sweet
country lullabies.
Pinky Johnson with
his violins, harmonicas.
I wore white shorts
and my legs glowed.
Why didn't I love
them then, taut as
wood still wondering
who would ask me
to dance, water lily
scent and roses,
special as Cotton Ave,

the Mocking Bird
song with its "kiss her
in the center if you
dare"

TALK TO ME

I think of Joni with
her silent man and
I'm wondering if
the ones I've picked
who don't talk come
from the silence of
my father, just a
shape at the end of
the table, a back
walking away. Now
there's a someone
who talks but keeps
who he is close.
No one knows about
him. He says nothing
on Facebook while
others babble away.
Maybe a map of his
latest joy. Who knows
if he's close to women
or men. Oh, he seems
kind and when he
teaches he's cool. He
seems easy in his skin
but I'd be a fool to
think I know him at
all. And then I think
of those who, as Joni
says, "spend every
sentence as if it was

marked currency"
when I've wanted
them to shut me up
with their face and
then talk to me

JERICO

trying to be friends with
an old lover, letting
go and still having
something to hold.
Where the images of
love that's paled?
I don't have many
today. It feels blah
as the gray rain upstate,
sticky and flat. Any
thing wild and
gentle that should
go running wild
kenneled in me

PAPRIKA PLAINS

I think of her going
backward in time,
back to her home
town floating off
film run backward
until her gray and
blond hair goes
sun and she's wide
eyed to everything.
She's in her mother's
arms and still it
keeps raining. I
imagine Jungle
Gardenia on her
fingers and thumbs
as the moon wanes
and waxes, I think of
her with time
ripped away

DREAMLAND

I think of her blonde
hair bleached, nearly
snow. Sun scorched
and her skin smelling
of coconut. I think
of island dreams,
sambas and trumpets,
heat dazed, dream
fazed, a lover's
tongue, a glass
of rum. Island colors,
guava, rose, peach and
avocado. Drunk on
sun and carnival music.
Licorice skin swaying.
Gambling and rambling.
White snow drifts
6 feet in New York City